Beginning Technique for the Cello

by Cassia Harvey

CHP110

©2004 by C. Harvey Publications® All Rights Reserved.
www.charveypublications.com - print books and free sheet music blog
www.learnstrings.com - PDF downloadable books and sheet music

Beginning Technique for the Cello

Practice Suggestions

1. Play with full bows and strong tone.

2. With the left hand, play on the tips of the fingers. Keep the fingers curved.

   Concentrate especially on the position of the 3rd and 4th fingers.

3. Press the strings down firmly and completely.

4. Take a short rest if your fingers get tired or if your hand hurts at all.

5. Start slowly. Only play faster when the notes are in tune.

6. Sit up straight and focus on good form.

Beginning Technique
WEEK 1

Cassia Harvey

Finger Exercise 1

©2004 C. Harvey Publications All Rights Reserved.

Double Stops 1

Playing two notes together makes a double stop.
Put your bow on two strings at the same time.

Bow Rhythms 1

Beginning Technique for the Cello

String Crossing 1

More Bow Rhythms

©2004 C. Harvey Publications All Rights Reserved.

WEEK 2

Finger Exercise 2

Double Stops 2

Bow Rhythms 2

String Crossing 2

Sliding Practice

Slide each finger to the end of the fingerboard and back.
Keep the finger round and strong as you slide.
Keep your elbow raised so you don't hit the side of the cello.

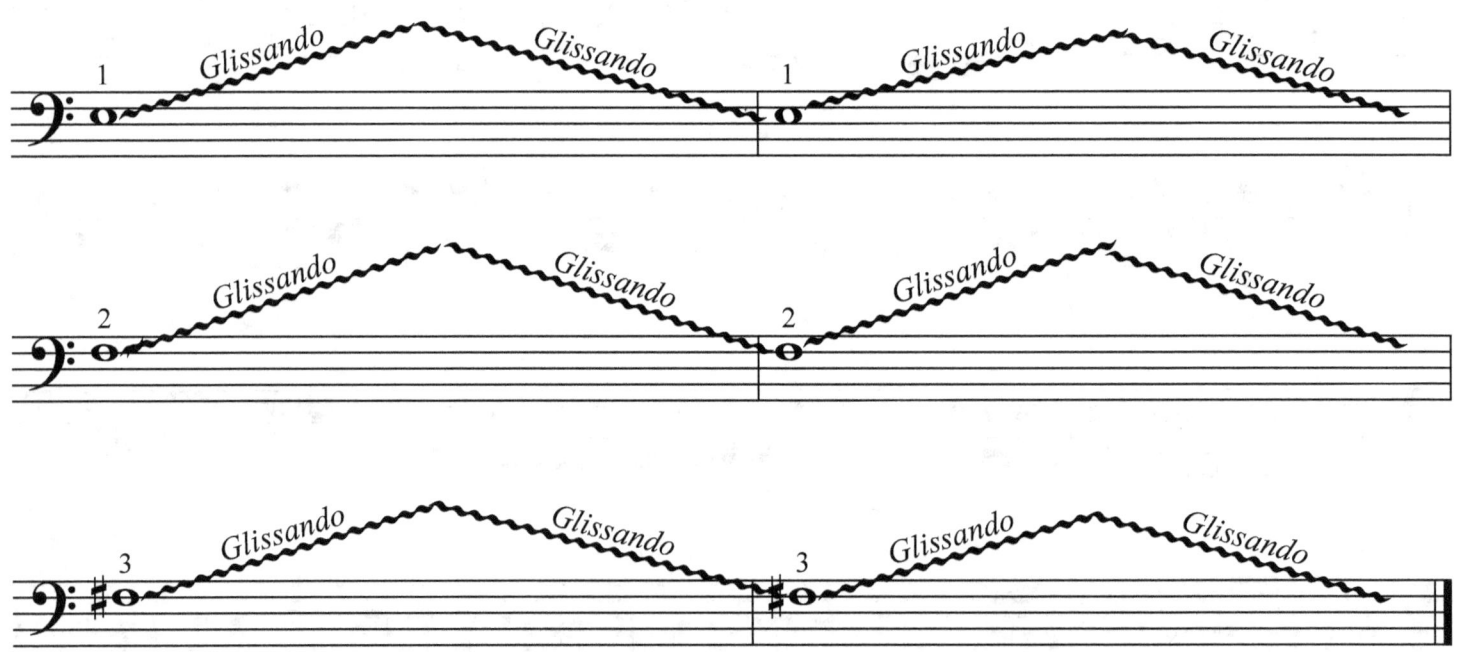

©2004 C. Harvey Publications All Rights Reserved.

Beginning Technique for the Cello

WEEK 3

Finger Exercise 3

©2004 C. Harvey Publications All Rights Reserved.

Double Stops 3

Bow Rhythms 3

WEEK 4

Finger Exercise 4

Double Stops 4

Bow Rhythms 4

String Crossing 4

Harmonics

Only put one finger on the string at a time.
Lift the other fingers in the air.
Touch the string very lightly.
Make sure your finger is in the right spot.

WEEK 5

Slurs

When you get to the middle of the bow, pick your finger up.

When you get to the middle of the bow, put your finger down.

Finger Exercise 5

Beginning Technique for the Cello

Double Stops 5

Grace Notes

WEEK 6

Slurs

Putting Fingers Down

Picking Fingers Up

Beginning Technique for the Cello

Finger Exercise 6

Scales for fingering practice

©2004 C. Harvey Publications All Rights Reserved.

Double Stops 6

Putting It All Together

Beginning Technique for the Cello

SCALES

D major

G major

C major, First Octave

C major, Second Octave

C major, Two Octaves

Broken Thirds and Arpeggios

D major

G major

C major

Beginning Technique for the Cello

F major

Broken Thirds and Arpeggios in F major

Cello Study: What's Next?

Work on Fingering and Bowing by Studying Scales
First Position Scale Studies for the Cello CHP179

Learn When to Use 2nd and 3rd Finger and Start Learning Extensions
Playing In Keys for Cello, Book One CHP242

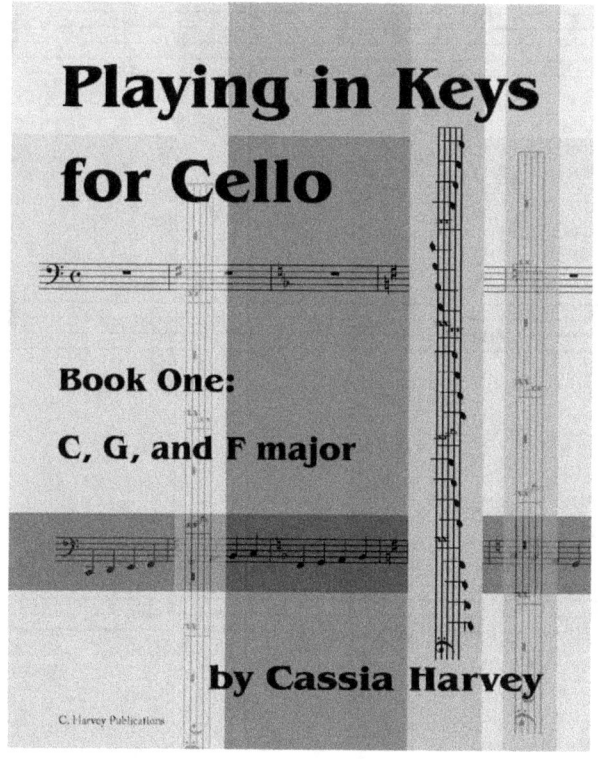
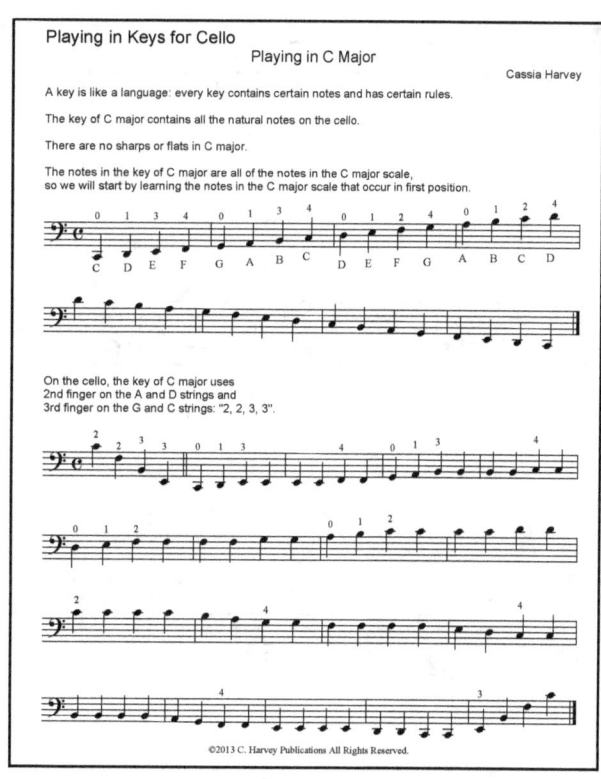

available from www.charveypublications.com: CHP243
Cello Stretching: Extended First Position

Part One: Stretching Back to a Flat

Cassia Harvey

In closed first position, the space between first and second fingers is a half step:

In order to reach some flats, the first finger extends back, while the other fingers remain in first position:

The 2nd, 3rd, and 4th fingers are in closed (regular) first position

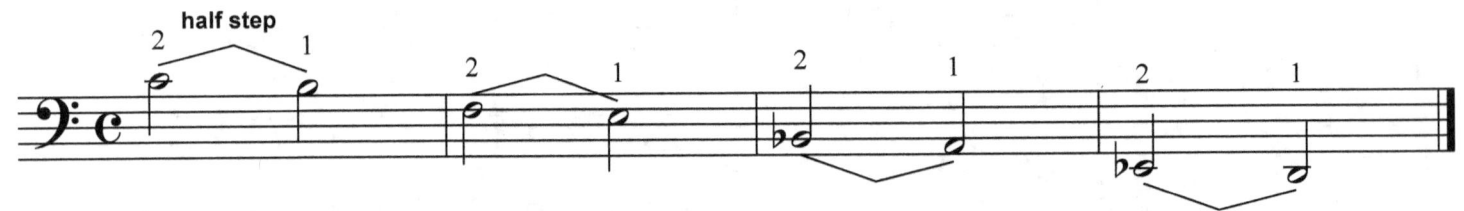

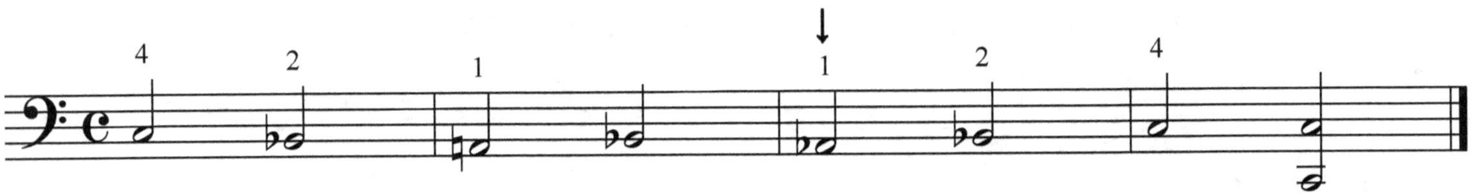

©2014 C. Harvey Publications All Rights Reserved.

www.ingramcontent.com/pod-product-compliance
Lightning Source LLC
Chambersburg PA
CBHW051430070526
44584CB00023B/3668